75 FAST & LEGAL WAYS TO MAKE QUICK CASH

BY OLIVIA MCDONALD, MBA

Can't make your rent payment this month? Having a problem putting gas in your car? If you've already exhausted all your available funds and usual sources of credit, here are 75 ways you can raise some cash in a hurry. These ideas range from mundane to desperate, and while I wouldn't necessarily encourage you to try them all, they are at least all legal and you can pick and choose the ones that work best for you.

Read through this exhaustive list, try the ones that interest you, and you should have more cash by next week. Although you may not want to do some of the things on this list long term, you can at least make some quick bucks to get you out of a short-term bind.

Full of ideas from traditional to modern, from no tech to high tech, you're sure to find some that work for you!

1

COLLECT YOUR CHANGE

When you're hard up for cash one of the first things you should do is collect your small change. Cash in your coin jar and search the usual places in your house for more. Check the bed stand, your home office, the sofa cushions, pockets, laundry room, junk drawer and your car.

SELL STUFF ON CRAIGSLIST

Over 50 million people search Craigslist every day and it's a great free place to list almost anything that you may have for sale. Go through your house and garage looking for things you no longer need or haven't used for a while, sell your old bicycles, furniture, musical equipment, art, housewares, even plants from your house and yard. Most Craigslist transactions are local and since the deals are done in person you don't have to ship anything and you get your cash immediately. Check out the pages for your local community to see the going prices and to get even more ideas of things you might want to sell.

3

SELL YOUR PLASMA

Most larger cities have clinics or blood banks that will pay you from around $30 to $50 for donating plasma and you can donate up to twice a week. It will take about an hour of your time to donate and you need to be drug free and relatively healthy to qualify. If you have a rare blood type you could potentially make even more money per donation.

SELL YOUR HAIR

Women or men with long hair can make anywhere from $40 to over a thousand dollars if you're willing to cut it off. Your hair must not be colored and should be at least ten inches long. Better quality hair without sun damage is worth more. Check out BuyAndSellHair.com or similar websites to see current prices and list yours for sale.

SELL YOUR BREAST MILK

Medical studies showing that breast milk has many benefits for babies have helped to create a large market for this "liquid gold" over the Internet. While largely unregulated, recent mothers with a plentiful supply of breast milk can go to OnlyTheBreast.com , basically the CraigsList of breast milk, and list theirs for sale. A month's supply can cost anywhere from $300 to $1,200.

SELL YOUR SPERM

Sperm banks will pay anywhere from $1 to $200 per week, with the average being about $40 per donation. You can typically deposit sperm every five days, so it could add up over time, but you may first have to wait through a month or more of tests before you start getting paid. You will likely never know what happened to your children, however this could be a relatively simple way to bring on some cash. Check out CryoBank.com or search the internet for other sperm banks.

BABYSIT

Lots of parents are in desperate need of a day or evening off from their kids. If you don't mind dealing with a few tantrums or spit ups, then babysitting can be a quick and easy way to bring in a few extra bucks. Reliable babysitters are in high demand and many earn upwards of $15 an hour so this can be a lucrative gig for you if you're good with kids. You can list your childcare, senior care and even pet care services at Care.com to get maximum exposure.

PET SIT

Boarding pets in your own home or taking care of them in the owner's home can be a lucrative gig. Offer to take care of people's pets while they're out of town, you'll likely be especially busy during the holidays. Kennels are usually pretty expensive plus they're impersonal and can be intimidating for pets so you could provide a nice alternative for pet lovers near you and you could even charge more during the holiday season when kennels fill up quickly. Try DogVacay.com to list your services.

HOUSE SIT

Offer to house sit for friends of friends, they're more likely to pay you for bringing in their mail and watering their plants than your close friends are since they may expect you to do those chores for free.

10

COUPONS

If one of the things you need cash for is to buy some groceries, then check out popular websites like ShopperStrategy.com and Hip2Save.com to search for deals and coupons you can use on things you'd be buying anyway. Every dollar you don't have to spend is a dollar back in your pocket!

11

RETURN PAST PURCHASES

An immediate way to make some quick cash is by taking any recently purchased items back to the store. If you've kept the receipts you should be able to get your full purchase price back, except for some items like electronics that may have a "restocking" fee. If you've made your purchases with a credit card, you'll only get a credit, but that could be a huge help in a pinch and you could even use the space you freed up on the credit card to pay your power bill if necessary.

12

RECYCLE SCRAP METAL

The price of metal has gone way up so you can get some quick cash by selling scrap metal to your local salvage yard or recycling center. Check your garage, shed, yard or basement for old pipes or other metal to salvage. If you have any old appliances sitting around this is a great way to clean out some junk and make a few bucks at the same time.

Look for discarded metal items in your neighborhood or ask your neighbors if you can help them get rid of an old swing set or help clear out their garages. You might even offer to split the proceeds with them if they'll help do the heavy lifting.

Computers are also full of valuable metals. For example, tower cases are usually made of steel and/or aluminum, plus the CPUs, RAM, motherboards, and PCIs all contain gold. You can find junk computers on CraigsList or offer to take outdated computers off the hands of a school or office doing upgrades so you can gather quite a few and sell them in bulk to make more money.

13

POOPER SCOOPER

If the thought of canine feces doesn't disgust you, then you might consider offering your services as a pooper scooper to neighbors with pets. Get out a shovel, some gloves and a bag and start knocking on a few doors.

14

COMPUTER REPAIR

For those with computer skills a part time computer repair business could bring in some much-needed cash. Offer to fix your friends' or neighbors' computers or help them upgrade or install software for a fee. You won't need any inventory and if you perform a valuable service you could get lots of referrals. You can even offer your computer support services, as well as wi-fi and network setup, TV installation and Smart Home setup services through sites like HelloTech.com.

15

ASK FOR A RAISE

An easy way to increase your income right away if you already have a job is to ask your boss for a raise. Let him or her know how long it has been since your last raise and be prepared to list some reasons why you are worth a little more money.

16

RENT OUT YOUR PARKING SPOT

If you live in a city where parking space is hard to come by, you might consider renting out your personal parking spot and start parking a little further away. Although it will be a little less convenient, you could put some nice extra cash in your pocket and get some exercise. Better yet, if you have one car and two spaces this could be a no brainer. There are numerous websites geared toward facilitating personal vehicle rentals like SpotHero.com, ParkingPanda.com and MoneyParking.co.

17

GET A PART-TIME JOB

When it comes to taking a part-time job, you should be aware that most of them won't get you paid too quickly since it could be two weeks or more before you receive your first paycheck. If you need some cash faster than that you should look for jobs with more immediate pay, like those that include tips such as bartending or waiting tables. You might even consider delivering pizzas, working at a hotel or driving a taxi.

18

MAKE THINGS TO SELL

If you're at all crafty you can break out your sewing machine or your glue gun and create some crafts to sell. Some other items to consider making include soaps, infused oils, or knitted scarves, although these things might take longer to complete. List your products on Etsy for some quick cash or set up a booth at a local festival or flea market to display your wares. This is an especially good gig for stay at home parents or others, who have gaps of free time to fill, just be sure to test the market for your items before you create a huge inventory of them to make sure they will sell.

BE A MECHANICAL TURK ON AMAZON

There are all sorts of ways to make extra cash on the Internet these days, some more legit than others. Amazon offers a method of raising some money for completing simple mundane tasks through their Mechanical Turk program. Companies post tasks that can't be easily done by machines that they need humans to do. You just sign up at Mturk.com, choose the assignments that interest you, and get credited with payment to your Amazon account upon completion. The money can be withdrawn once you accumulate $10, but the payouts for assignments can be pretty low.

HOLD A YARD SALE

How much money you can raise at a yard sale depends on what and how much you have to sell, your advertising, and the weather, but it can be a very quick way to make a few hundred extra bucks. Make some signs to put out on main roads near you at least a day or two in advance, place an ad on Cragslist and check your local newspaper to see if they have free ads for yard sales. Consider asking your neighbors if they'd like to have a yard sale the same weekend to draw more traffic and ask them to chip in for an ad if you have to pay for one. My neighborhood holds a community yard sale a couple times a year and we all went in together to buy a vinyl banner that we place at the subdivision entrance each time we hold a sale.

21

SEEK EMERGENCY ASSISTANCE

There are public and private agencies that provide emergency assistance. Although they don't usually provide cash and they often restrict their assistance to those below the poverty level, many provide items and services that you would otherwise spend money on so they could help you free up some cash. The most common types of assistance include food banks, food stamps, clothing, household essentials and waivers or help with utility bills.

Check your local government offices for social services and look into churches and social clubs with outreach programs. Try searching the Internet for your city + social services or public assistance. It can be humbling to ask for charity, but if you are having a tough time this is always an option.

CROWD FUNDING

If you have a specific expense you need help with, say medical bills, or a plane ticket to visit your sick mother, then you may consider asking for donations through crowd funding sites like Fundly, GoFundMe or KickStarter.

BECOME A TEMP

Sign up with a temporary employee agency near you, there are different types that specialize in office workers, day laborers and other types of employment. Temp jobs typically pay really well, and you'll get paid quickly, although they don't usually provide any benefits. While I was in college, I would check in with my favorite temp agency every time I came home for a long break to earn some extra money and it was amazing how often I was offered a permanent job at the companies I temped for.

24

SIGN UP FOR MEDICAL TESTS

Many large universities have ongoing medical research projects where they use test subjects to help evaluate the efficacy of new treatments and medicines. Because the number of people willing to volunteer to test the medications is usually pretty small, they provide cash compensation that typically ranges from a few hundred to over a thousand dollars. Search the Internet for medical test volunteers to find some programs near you. Test participants should be reasonably healthy and generally will at least get a free physical.

BE A PART TIME DRIVER

With so many personal taxi and services these days, you could earn some quick cash by becoming an Uber or Lyft driver. These companies allow you to use your personal vehicle to earn an income by driving others around town and you can even earn money for referring other drivers.

DELIVER FOOD

Companies like Uber and Lyft have restrictions about the age and condition of your vehicle so if for some reason you do not meet those requirements to drive passengers around you could still deliver food for Uber Eats, Waitr or DoorDash. In some cases, if your area permits, all you need is a bicycle to get paid for making food deliveries.

SELL AD SPACE ON YOUR CAR

You can sign up with companies like Stickr.co to sell advertising space on the back window of your vehicle. Once you sign up you can select the type of ad you want to display and they send you a decal for the window that you can see through from the inside. Apply the decal to your window and submit a picture of it each month to confirm it is still on your vehicle and the company says you can make up to $495 per month for simply driving as you would normally.

GET A ROOMMATE

If you have an extra bedroom in your home or apartment, then sharing living expenses can put more cash in your pocket. Be sure to sign a lease agreement, even if the prospective tenant is someone you know. Discuss how you will share common living areas like the kitchen and bathroom(s) beforehand, as well as how shared bills like power and water will be handled, to cut down on any issues later.

TAP INTO YOUR LIFE INSURANCE

Most whole life or universal insurance policies build up cash value over time and you can take out the cash or 'borrow' against the policy if you desperately need some funds. Read the details in your policy or call the agency to ask questions about how much you can take out and how you go about doing that. If you've only had the policy for a short time there may not be much to take out, but if you've had it a long while you could be pleasantly surprised at how much has accumulated. This is a reasonable option if you're still young and healthy but be aware that if you have health issues it could be difficult or costly to get a replacement policy later.

RAID YOUR IRA

Your retirement savings account can be a great place to get a lump sum of cash if you're really in need, but make sure you understand the rules. If you don't qualify for an eligible withdrawal you'll have to pay a 10% penalty plus taxes on the money at your current income tax rate. Also keep in mind that it's difficult to replace any retirement funds and you'll lose the opportunity to earn interest on the funds that you take out.

31

GET A PAYDAY LOAN

Although not a highly recommended option, you could take out a payday loan if you're in need of some quick cash and you'll be able to pay it back in a short period of time. However, if you're not responsible with your money or don't think you can pay it off right away, then payday loans can become a vicious cycle and will make your money problems even worse. If you feel like you must resort to a payday loan then take along proof of employment and a photo ID like your driver's license.

32

PAWN YOUR
VALUABLE ITEMS

Pawn shops offer loans against items that you
bring in as collateral. The shop will make you a
loan offer based on what they think is the value
of the item, usually about 10% of the actual
value, and give you a set of amount of time to
pay back the loan. If you agree to the offer but
don't pay it back with interest in time, generally
a month, then the loan expires, and the pawn
shop gets to keep or sell the goods. The benefit
of a pawn shop loan over a payday loan is that
there is nothing more to pay if you default so
you don't have to worry about interest
compounding or going any deeper into debt,
plus its immediate cash and you don't have the
hassle of selling your things on eBay or
Craigslist.

33

SET UP A ROADSIDE STAND

Put up a stand on a busy roadway and sell some goods. Examples include selling bottled water at a freeway exit, selling flower bouquets in front of a corner store, fruit and vegetables along the highway or hawking baked goods at the entrance to a busy subdivision. The trick is to find a legal location with a good traffic flow where people can park easily and pick high profit items to sell. Also check to see if a vendor's license is required.

34

SCALP TICKETS

If you're broke and you really need money, but you happen to have tickets to an upcoming concert or musical, consider selling your tickets to recoup your cash, you might even be able to make a little profit if the event is sold out. Check the restrictions on the tickets and your state laws. In general, it is legal to resell tickets, but some states have restrictions against making a profit off the sale. You could list them on eBay and the site will let you know if it is allowed in your state, or visit StubHub.com to list them for sale. Alternatively, if it is sold out, you could go stand outside on the night of the event and try to sell your tickets there. Show up early and you may even find a professional scalper to buy them from you.

RECYCLE ALUMINUM CANS

Start collecting your own empty soda cans and go scavenging for more. Keep a couple of plastic bags in your car and look for cans along ditch lines and in parking lots, you could even ask friends, co-workers and neighbors to save theirs for you. Current prices run about 42 cents a pound and most recycling plants will pay more if you bring in over 50 pounds. It takes 32 cans to make a pound and you'll make even more in states that require a deposit like California and Michigan.

VISIT A CASINO

When visiting a casino you <u>must</u> keep in mind that the house always has the advantage so this is not the best idea if you're already short on cash, but I'm listing it here because it does have the potential of turning some cash into more cash. Avoid games that are 100% luck like slot machines and roulette and opt instead for games of skill like blackjack or video poker, but only if you know what you're doing. If you do decide to go this route then make yourself a promise before you enter that you'll quit as soon as you have the money you need and decide on a loss limit before you go.

SELL STOCK PHOTOS

Taking and selling stock photos is a terrific way to make some passive income. If you have a decent camera and a little bit of talent you can take pictures with good lighting and composition and sell them online through stock photo websites. Photos of locations, people, even common items like park benches, trees, and food are easy to take and people buy them for use on websites, articles and marketing materials.

Images of people doing everyday things like kissing, fighting, laughing or even just sitting typically sell for more but you should be sure to get their written legal consent to sell the pictures. Here are some reputable sites where you can sell your photos:

123RF.com
BigStockPhoto.com
CanStockPhoto.com

CorbisImages.com
DepositPhotos.com
DreamsTime.com
Fotolia.com
iStockPhoto.com
ShutterPoint.com
ShutterStock.com
ThinkStockPhotos.com

SCAVENGE FOR VALUABLES

Go scavenging for valuables that you can sell. Grab your metal detector or borrow one and go to public places like the beach, parks or parking lots where people typically drop or lose things like jewelry, coins and other goods.

FLIP PRODUCTS

When people flip houses they typically buy "fixer uppers" and repair them so they can then sell them for a profit. Of course, flipping houses takes a big investment of both time and money so I'm not suggesting you do that, but you can buy other things and then sell them for more. Check out yard sales, thrift stores and police auctions for items that you can grab for a bargain and resell for a profit.

UPDATE USED FURNITURE

You could also breathe new life into old thrift store furniture by repairing and refinishing it and make a profit that way. One of my brothers makes a steady side income doing this, he looks for old furniture with "good bones" on Craigslist and at yard sales, he's even been known to pick up castoffs waiting for trash collection on the side of the road, then replaces drawer pulls and other hardware and updates the furniture with new paint then sells the pieces through a furniture consignment store. He's even made tables from old wooden doors and planters from wine bottles. Use your imagination and the options are endless.

41

RESELL WHOLESALE ITEMS

If you're able to get a deal on some wholesale items you could sell them for a profit online or locally by setting up a booth at festivals. Items that typically sell well at festivals include sunglasses, purses, hats and t-shirts but you could search for wholesale deals on any products that interest you. Be sure to research the going prices and market demand for the items so you'll understand the profit margins. This way you will not overpay on the wholesale end or be left with lots of product that you cannot move.

MONEYMAKING APPS ON YOUR PHONE

You can actually get paid to do small tasks via apps on your phone. There are a number of apps that will pay you for doing things like scanning products at the grocery store or submitting pictures of your receipts after shopping and other marketing-oriented gigs. Check out these apps that will pay you back:

AppTrailers.com
CashKingApp.com
CheckPoints.com
EasyShiftApp.com
FieldAgent.net
GigWalk.com
Gym-Pact.com
iBotta.com
IconZoomer.com
JunoWallet.com

NPolls.com
ShopKick.com
Staree.com

43

FILL OUT ONLINE SURVEYS

Online surveys typically pay only a few dollars apiece so you won't get rich this way, but they also require very little effort and can be done while you watch television or in your free time. Surveyors are generally looking for specific age groups or types of people so you won't qualify for all of them, but there are many out there to choose from.

You'll be asked to fill out some information when you register so the survey companies can send you the ones that you do qualify for. Sign up with several different companies to get more offers then watch your email and check the sites regularly for survey opportunities.

You don't have to complete any surveys that you don't want to do, but obviously the more you do the more you'll get paid. Remember, you should never have to pay to join a survey site and look for ones that either pay in cash or points that can be converted to cash. You might also want to consider setting up a separate email for your survey accounts to avoid getting any spam in your regular account. Following is a list of legitimate survey sites:

BigSpot.com
GetPaidSurveys.com
GlobalTestMarket.com
i-Say.com
InboxDollars.com
MyPoints.com
MySurvey.com
NCPsignup.com
SurveyPolice.com
SwagBucks.com
Toluna.com
Vindale.com
ZoomPanel.com

ANSWER QUESTIONS

You can turn your knowledge into cash by answering questions online. There are several different websites where users can ask questions on all sorts of topics like computers, cars, law, medicine, cooking, relationships and more general topics, and people get paid for answering them. You probably know something about a lot of different things or have lots of experience in an area that you could help others with. Check out these websites to get a feel for the topics and payouts:

AceYourCollegeClasses.com
ChaCha.com
Ether.com
HelpOwl.com
JustAnswer.com
Keen.com
Mahalo.com

Pearl.com
Rewarder.com
SmallBizAdvice.com
StudentOfFortune.com
WebAnswers.com
WerLive.com

TEST MOBILE APPS AND WEBSITES

Sign up at UserTesting.com to test web and mobile sites for $10 to $15 each by downloading an application that asks you to perform specific tasks on a site. You'll be asked a few questions about your experience and the application will record your screen and voice while you're using the site. While it may not be a steady income, it could put some much-needed cash in your pocket.

JOIN A FOCUS GROUP

You can participate in online or in-person focus groups, like those performed by 20/20 Panel where they pay from $50 to $150 or more for giving your opinion on all sorts of things for research or marketing studies. You can also search for local focus groups at FindFocusGroups.com. Focus groups are typically more in depth than the surveys you can do online but they also pay better. Here are some other similar sites you may want to look at:

2020Research.com
eJury.com
OnlineVerdict.com

GET A MICRO-JOB

Micro-jobs are small tasks that you do for compensation and there are a number of sites online where you can pick up these jobs. TaskRabbit lists local jobs like assembling furniture, picking up CraigsList purchases, grocery shopping or meal pickup for people and simple business tasks. At Fiverr you can offer services like graphics and design, writing and translation, music and audio, video and animation and others, all starting from at least $5 each. GigWalk is an iPhone app that lets you take on "gigs" in your area such as taking a picture of a local business, sign or point of purchase display for a few dollars or more each.

SELL YOUR COIN COLLECTION

If you've been collecting coins for a while, chances are that you have some worth selling at your local coin shop. You can also hunt for pre-1982 pennies as they contain more copper than newer ones that are alloyed with zinc and are worth more than a cent apiece. A good technique is buy rolls of pennies at the bank, sort them to find the older coins, then exchange the ones you don't want and buy more rolls. You could also hunt for pre-1964 silver half dollars. They are worth more than fifty cents apiece because they contain 90% silver. Like with the pennies, you can buy rolls of half dollars at the bank and keep only the most valuable ones.

SELL YOUR STAMP COLLECTION

I'd been collecting mint sheets of stamps for quite a while and since they've never been used they're worth at least as much as their face value, but I was surprised to find out how much more valuable they are than their actual face value since they're in great condition and are no longer being printed. If you have any sort of a stamp collection you might get lucky and find some that are worth selling. Check out prices online at TheSwedishTiger.com, look at stamp catalogs at your local library or visit a nearby dealer to find out what yours are worth.

BECOME A MOVING ADVERTISEMENT

Some companies will pay you to "wrap" your car in an advertisement or drive around with their bumper stickers. You could even get paid to wear t-shirts, clothes, or costumes that advertise a business. In addition to receiving a free t-shirt, you can get paid for every day that you wear the shirt to a public, conspicuous place, or get paid to hold up a sale sign on the side of a road for a local business. Ask around at nearby real estate offices, restaurants and stores to see what you might be able to do for them.

51

DO ODD JOBS

Are you handy with tools? You could offer to do repairs for people in your neighborhood. If you have a reliable vehicle you could pick up groceries or run errands for people. Put a notice on CraigsList or pass out flyers advertising your services. There are often ads on CraigsList and in the newspaper looking for people to help with painting, moving, mowing and other quick labor jobs. You can also list your services on sites like Handy.com, LawnLove.com and YourMechanic.com.

CREATE RECIPES FOR CASH

If you are good in the kitchen and can take pictures, then create some recipes, take pictures of each step, and sell the recipes and images to bloggers looking for content. You will find Facebook groups full of content providers who write articles, make crafts and create recipes for bloggers. Here are a couple places to check out for ideas - Blogger Resource Room, Pinterest Friendly Content for Bloggers and Let's Get Creative are just a few of the private Facebook groups you can join to sell your recipes.

BE A STREET PERFORMER

If you have a talent then you can dance, play music, mime, sing, or tell jokes on a busy public street to make some cash as a performer. You probably shouldn't do this unless you are actually good at it, but if you put together a good act and can find a place to perform hopefully people will reward you with tips for entertaining them. Be sure to check local regulations and bylaws regarding performing in a public space.

TUTOR STUDENTS

If its exam season you could find lots of desperate students to tutor if you have knowledge of common subjects to share like math, science, history and languages. Help a few people pass their exams and make some money at the same time. Although exam time is great for a tutoring business, you can get started anytime you'd like. Advertise your services campus bulletin boards, online and on street boards or posts. Go to campuses and find their bulletin boards and pin up your offer.

CREDIT CARD REWARDS

Many credit cards have rewards programs that pay you back in cash or points that you can use to buy things like gift cards. Check with your credit card companies to see if there are any vouchers you can claim that may cover things you need to purchase.

DOG WALKING

Lots of people own dogs but have very busy lives and aren't always available to walk them so they'll enjoy the chance to pay you for walking their dogs. Make up a flyer and start knocking on doors or pin up a flyer on the bulletin board at nearby grocery and pet stores. Once you build up a clientele, you'll be able to walk several dogs at once and earn even more money in the same amount of time.

SELL USED BOOKS

There are several websites that buy used books and you can start by searching your home for books that you've already read or no longer need. Simply type in the ISBN numbers to see if the site is buying that particular book and how much they will pay you for them. Most will pay the shipping and send you a box to ship the books in if you need one. Some even have apps for your cell phone that allow you to scan the ISBN numbers to get the price quicker. You can use the app at garage sales and flea markets to see if the books you find there are worth more than the asking price so you could buy them and turn around and resell them for a profit. These are my favorite book buyers:

BookScouter.com
eCampus.com
SellBackYourBook.com

SELL YOUR USED ELECTRONICS

If you're like most of us, you probably have your previous model cell phone in a drawer somewhere, or an old tablet you don't use anymore laying around. Sites like Gazelle.com and uSell.com will pay you cash for your used electronics. Simply select your make, model and current condition from the drop-down lists and you'll instantly be given an offer for your item. If you accept the offer, you'll be given mailing instructions and payment is typically made as soon as the item is received.

BARGAIN-HUNT AT YARD AND THRIFT SALES

If you have a bit of knowledge in a particular area (ex. Comic books, action figures, jewelry, classic National Geographics) or even just a good eye for a bargain, visit private sales early and often to find unexpected deals that you can resell. My mom has a neighbor who makes some steady side cash buying up good used jeans at yard and thrift sales then reselling them at consignment shops.

GO TO POLICE AUCTIONS

There are incredible deals to be found at police auctions, and while you may not be able to resell a car that was involved in a serious crime, you can probably typically find some outstanding deals on cheap jewelry and electronics that will easy for you to resell for a profit.

61

FLIP USED CARS

If you're mechanically inclined and pretty handy with a wrench you could buy decent used cars that need repairs, fix them up and resell them for a profit. I have a friend who does this routinely whenever he needs some cash, he'll buy a car that needs work from someone who can't afford to fix it, make the necessary repairs and then resell it for usually two or three times his cost. Keep in mind that you'll need the space and tools to do the repairs. Also, look for vehicles that can be repaired quickly so you get your initial investment back as soon as possible.

RESCUE BATTERED WOOD

Pallets are cheap (or free) and easy to come by. Look for used pallets construction sites, buildings under renovation, and shipping warehouses. You can make beautiful furniture or artwork from the used pallets to sell.

Additionally, you could plane down the boards and/or kiln-dry them in a homemade kiln-dryer to uncover their hidden beauty and then resell the wood. Noting that the wood is "reclaimed," when you market it can actually help bring better prices as people are often willing to pay much more for this.

WEB DESIGN

Put your web design and HTML skills to use if you have talent in that area and build websites for local small businesses, groups, and hobby clubs. Check with your friends who have side businesses to see if they need any help getting a website off the ground. Charge slightly lower than the going rate and you'll both benefit, especially since you don't have any overhead like rent for office space, just use your personal computer and Internet access that you already pay for.

BECOME A VIRTUAL ASSISTANT

A virtual assistant is someone who offers remote services to other businesses in exchange for an agreed upon fee. All you need to become a virtual assistant is an email address, an Internet connection and a few administrative skills like customer support, schedule management, transcription, research or bookkeeping. The list of services you could provide is lengthy and you don't have to provide every service out there, just choose the ones that appeal to you. Offer your services through sites like Fiverr.com and FancyHands.com, blogger groups on Facebook and/or your own website.

TEACH OTHERS TO SEW

If you're skilled with a sewing machine, needle and thread you could offer to teach others to sew for a fee. Sewing is becoming a lost art and there are people out there willing to pay to learn. You could organize classes for multiple students at a time at your local community center, church or YMCA or you could offer individual instruction in your home or the students' home.

CLOTHING ALTERATIONS

People are always in need of having their pants hemmed, waists taken in, buttons replaced, and seams repaired. If you're skilled with a sewing machine and know how to perform clothing alterations, you could come up with a rate list and offer your services on local community billboards or sites like CraigsList. Alternatively, you could visit local dry cleaners and offer a weekly pickup and drop off of clothes to be altered along with a rate split of say 70/30 (you get 70% for doing the work and they get 30% for selling the job) so that everyone benefits and you get a steady supply of work.

HOUSE OR CONDO CLEANING

Check out the "gigs" section on CraigsList for people needing their house or condo cleaned. You could also put up your own "gig" listing to offer house cleaning services. Check with local property management companies or people you know with AirBnB rentals as they're always in need of cleaning help. Pay should be a minimum of about $15 per hour depending on your location and you get the benefit of a flexible schedule.

DETAIL CARS

Love cars but you're not very mechanically inclined? If you can professionally detail a car you can earn pretty good fees offering these services to others. Print up some fliers and deliver them door to door in your neighborhood or visit local office buildings with the fliers and offer to perform your services in the parking lot while the customer goes about their regular workday. You may need to invest in a portable canopy if not performing your services in a garage or under a carport. Also, check with your local licensing authority to see if a license is required to offer car detailing services.

JOIN AIRBNB

Make your assets work for you if you have a spare room or two in your house, garage apartment, or other type of living space on your property and offer to rent it out on AirBnB. While having strangers stay in your home isn't for everyone, if you don't mind the company or keeping everything clean for guests, this can be a great way to make some extra money without too much effort on your part. Check out the AirBnB site for details and going rates in your area.

Of course there are other home rental sites available like VRBO.com, HomeAway.com and FlipKey.com. Check them all out and see which is the best fit for you and your property.

FREELANCE PROOFREADER

Your love of words and good grammar skills can help you earn a steady income as a freelance proofreader for court reporters, authors and bloggers. Check out ProofreadAnywhere.com to learn some professional skills that can help you grab lucrative court report transcription jobs. Since you can even provide transcription proofreading services from an iPad you could literally do this job from anywhere while traveling.

71

DELIVER
NEWSPAPERS

With a reliable vehicle and the ability to work
early morning hours you could make a decent
side income delivering newspapers. Call the
circulation department for your local newspaper
to check out the requirements and see if they're
hiring. Depending on the size of the route you
should be able to make from $150 to $500 per
week.

POWER WASHING

Do you own a power washer and enjoy working outdoors? If so, you could make some quick side cash by power washing driveways, sidewalks and curbs for your neighbors and others. Print up some flyers offering to power wash a front porch or patio for free with the purchase of a driveway for say $150. Be sure that whatever you charge covers the cost of supplies as well as your time plus a little profit of course.

73

DRIVE FOR AMAZON FLEX

As Amazon continues to grow rapidly and outgrow their usual shippers they've begun to hire their own local delivery people through the Amazon Flex program. Using just your car and a smartphone you can make $18-$25 an hour delivering packages for Amazon and you even get to set your own hours.

RENT OUT YOUR VEHICLE

Did you know you can make money renting out your car, boat, RV, bike or almost anything else? If your car is parked all day while you're at work or if you have an extra vehicle sitting around you can rent it out by the hour or the day through sites like Turo.com or HyreCar.com.

Rent out the RV that's been hanging out in your driveway through RVShare.com or rent your boat when you're not using it through Sailo.com. Cyclists, snow and water sport enthusiasts can rent our their bikes, skis, snowboards, paddleboards, kayaks and surfboards through SpinLister.com.

And, so that you airplane owners don't feel left out, you can rent out your plane when you're not using it through OpenAirplane.com.

DELIVER GROCERIES

Plenty of people are either too busy to pick up their own groceries or otherwise can't get to the grocery store themselves. The grocery delivery business is booming these days and you could make some extra cash (and the possibility of tips) by delivering groceries for services like InstaCart.com and Shipt.com.

www.ingramcontent.com/pod-product-compliance
Lightning Source LLC
Chambersburg PA
CBHW020605220526

45463CB00006B/2462